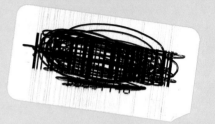

Taming and Training Cockatiels
KW-001

Contents

Photographers: Dr. Gerald R. Allen, Glen S. Axelrod, Dr. Herbert R. Axelrod, H. Bielfeld, Sam Fehrenz, Isabelle Francais, Michael Gilroy, E. Goldfinger, Ray Hanson, Jack Harris, B. Kahl, Harry V. Lacey, Bruce D. Lavoy, P. Leysen, J. Maier, R. and V. Moat, Fritz Prenzel, Nancy Richmond, San Diego Zoo, Brian Seed, Vince Serbin, George Smith, Vogelpark Walsrode, Dr. Matthew M. Vriends.

Overleaf: Male and female cockatiels. **Title page:** Headstudy of a cockatiel.

Distributed in the UNITED STATES by T.F.H. Publications, Inc., One T.F.H. Plaza, Neptune City, NJ 07753; in CANADA to the Pet Trade by H & L Pet Supplies Inc., 27 Kingston Crescent, Kitchener, Ontario N2B 2T6; Rolf C. Hagen Ltd., 3225 Sartelon Street, Montreal 382 Quebec; in CANADA to the Book Trade by Macmillan of Canada (A Division of Canada Publishing Corporation), 164 Commander Boulevard, Agincourt, Ontario M1S 3C7; in ENGLAND by T.F.H. Publications Limited, Cliveden House/Priors Way/Bray, Maidenhead, Berkshire SL6 2HP, England; in AUSTRALIA AND THE SOUTH PACIFIC by T.F.H. (Australia) Pty. Ltd., Box 149, Brookvale 2100 N.S.W., Australia; in NEW ZEALAND by Ross Haines & Son, Ltd., 18 Monmouth Street, Grey Lynn, Auckland 2, New Zealand; in SINGAPORE AND MALAYSIA by MPH Distributors (S) Pte., Ltd., 601 Sims Drive, #03/07/21, Singapore 1438; in the PHILIPPINES by Bio-Research, 5 Lippay Street, San Lorenzo Village, Makati Rizal; in SOUTH AFRICA by Multipet Pty. Ltd., 30 Turners Avenue, Durban 4001. Published by T.F.H. Publications, Inc. Manufactured in the United States of America by T.F.H. Publications, Inc.

TAMING AND TRAINING COCKATIELS

RISA TEITLER
PROFESSIONAL TRAINER

Preface

This book is intended as a manual for the inexperienced bird owner. The information is not meant to be taken as the last word on cockatiel taming, nutrition and breeding; it is, however, the result of many years of professional experience in breeding and handling these birds. If you follow the information and develop a training and feeding schedule, you will undoubtedly enjoy owning a healthy, happy cockatiel.

Cockatiels are one of the most easily tamed caged birds. They fit well into the lifestyles of most people. Remember that you can learn the most about taming a bird by doing it yourself, but read the material given here and whatever else you can find on the subject. Talk to experienced people and those who own cockatiels. Use your common sense and don't accept unqualifiedly any advice that contradicts your own judgment.

Congratulations on acquiring your first, or possibly one of many, cockatiels, and please remember that you can't train a sick cockatiel, so pay attention to the following pages.

Risa Teitler

*Opposite: Headstudy of a normal adult male cockatiel. **Right:** Cockatiels are among the most easily tamed cage bird species.*

Introduction

Cockatiels, sometimes called quarrion birds in their native Australia, are steadily gaining popularity as caged birds. They are called "Cockies" by many professionals. Their availability, relative low cost, affectionate personalities and talent for mimicry recommend them as family pets.

In the wild state, cockatiels are found throughout the Australian sub-continent, traveling in pairs or small flocks. They feed on seedling grasses, fruits, berries, grains and, to the dismay of farmers, on cultivated crops. Migration of the birds is apparently linked to the supply of fresh water. Breeding generally occurs between August and September (Australian winter) but may vary considerably according to climatic changes.

Approximately twelve inches long from graceful crest to slender tail, their plumage is predominantly grey, with a wide band of white on the wing. Mature males display a bright yellow head with orange patches over the ears. The upper side of the tail is pearl grey, the underside is black. Immatures and females are distinguished by the yellow and black banding on the underside of the tail, with facial yellow restricted to outlining the features. Young males begin to show color changes by six months of age. Once the first yellow feathers appear on the face, the entire head rapidly goes yellow.

Cockies are hardy birds with a

*Below: In the wild, cockatiels feed on seedling grasses, fruits, and berries. **Opposite:** The cockatiel is sometimes considered to be a relative of the cockatoo, a much larger bird.*

Above: Cockatiels are bred in several distinct color varieties. There is little difference, between birds of different colors, in their qualities as pets, and the difference in cost depends only upon the rarity of the color. *Opposite:* A normally colored cockatiel.

life expectancy of 20 to 25 years. Aviculturists have produced some new varieties in addition to the normal grey bird. These include the lutino or white cockatiel, first established as a reliable strain by Mrs. E.L. Moon; the pied, a beautiful bird with irregular patterns of white, grey and yellow all over the body; the pearly; the cinnamon; and the silver cockatiel. More color mutations are appearing regularly.

Once you have decided that a cockatiel is the bird for you, go to a few local pet dealers and see what they have to offer. Chances are you'll find the right bird at a reasonable cost. Now evaluate your ability as a trainer. Are you patient, calm and determined to win the friendship of your new bird? If you fit this description, you are almost assured of success. Cockatiels are ideal first birds for the young fancier, man or woman, who desires an amiable companion that requires a minimum of space and a simple diet. It is not a pet for young, irresponsible children to abuse.

Only one person should deal

One of the most popular cockatiel color mutations is the pearly cockatiel. The market for colored cockatiels continues to grow each year.

Cockatiels are ideal pets for people looking to acquire their first feathered friend, and they are challenging enough for those with avian experience.

with the bird initially in the taming situation. Choose the most motivated family member with the greatest amount of time to devote to taming the bird. Once the bird is hand-tame, the other household members should endeavor to establish their own relationships with the cockatiel or he may develop into a one-man bird.

Decide on a suitable location for the cage. Keep it out of the

Above: A lutino, or white, cockatiel. Opposite: The cinnamon cockatiel strain is a recent development of cockatiel breeders.

kitchen, where temperatures may fluctuate, and away from windows and other drafty spots. Placement near the door also subjects the bird to drafts, and if he flies away, the danger of escape is obvious. In cold climates, avoid housing the bird near radiators or heaters, since the dry heat may be detrimental. Some bird owners devote an entire room to their pets, and if this is the case, the room can be designed especially for birds. Others allow their pets to fly free in a screened patio area, but care must be taken to bring them indoors in cold or rainy weather.

Outdoor aviaries for cockatiels are fine if adequate shelter from the elements is provided. The outdoor situation presents special problems for the bird owner in the form of neighborhood cats, dogs, and rodents that may eat the food provided for the birds. In addition,

When you first bring your pet cockatiel home, only one person should work with it until it is hand-tame. Later, other family members can work with the bird.

Cockatiels love to chew; therefore, they should be provided with enough material upon which to gnaw. If they don't have something suitable to chew on, they will find something else.

more attention must be given to keeping the birds free of pests such as feather mites and lice, which are rarely present on a caged house pet.

Outside, free flying for the cockatiel should be considered only if you are located far from busy streets and have property where no other residences are within sight or sound. Establish a definite feeding station and time, and, as an added draw, you may want to acquire a second cockatiel to keep caged in full sight of the free bird. First, introduce the yard to a clipped bird. Give him every opportunity to familiarize himself with the surroundings. By the time his flight feathers have been replaced, he should consider himself part owner of the property and will have little inclination to leave. Again, a feeding area with plenty of fresh water and a regular feeding schedule will help train a

Headstudy of a healthy immature female. Note the full crest, the clear eye, and the clean nostrils.

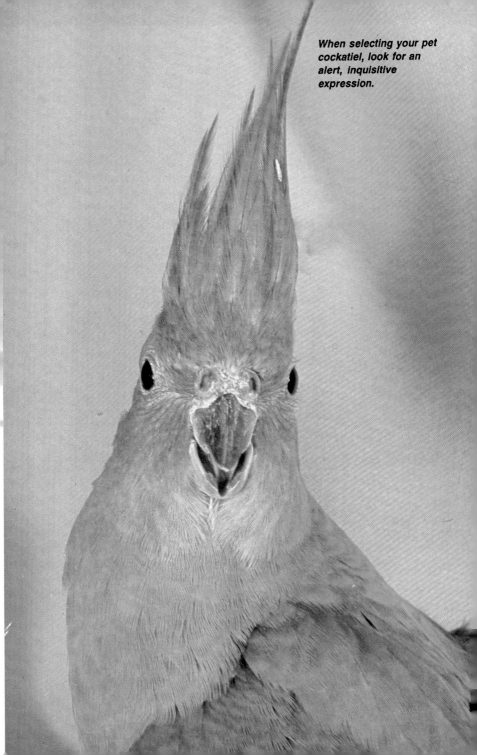

When selecting your pet cockatiel, look for an alert, inquisitive expression.

Your pet cockatiel, no matter how tame it becomes, should be properly supervised at all times, as potential dangers lurk everywhere.

free flyer to remain close to home. Don't expect to establish a free flyer in a short time. The whole process may take from a few months to a year. For most people, in fact, it is not a good idea at all to try to establish cockatiels as free flyers; there are too many dangers.

CHOOSING THE BIRD

Many people feel that it is necessary to buy two cockatiels, because one bird will be lonely. On the contrary, if what you want is a tame pet bird, you should buy only one. A single bird is more easily tamed and taught to talk.

Now that you've decided on one bird or two, look for a pet dealer that has a clean shop, clean cages and feeders, and employees that are able to answer your questions satisfactorily.

Availability of good quality feed and supplies, including cages, stands, toys and books, may be other factors that influence your choice of a pet shop.

The best candidate for an easily tamed pet is a young bird between ten and 16 weeks of age. Obviously, a cockatiel that already shows a bright yellow head is at least six months old, and although it is possible to make a fine pet out of an older bird, it is much more difficult and time consuming. The purchase of a colored out (mature) bird has one advantage: there can be no mistake about the sex of the bird. Both males and females make good pets and can acquire speech, but the male cockatiel is usually a better talker.

If you are lucky enough to find a pet dealer that offers hand-reared young, take advantage of the situation, for the bird will be tame when you get it. Otherwise make

A lutino cockatiel. Some lutinos have red eyes, and some have black eyes.

Above: Cockatiels need to chew on calcium blocks of some sort. These two birds are gnawing on a cuttlebone, made from the bone of a cuttlefish. Opposite: Move slowly and deliberately when placing your hand in the bird's cage.

Opposite: Try to choose a young cockatiel for taming and training. Young cockatiels do not have the bright coloration of the adult birds. Right: A mature lutino cockatiel.

your choice on the basis of the following criteria.

Buy a healthy bird. Judge its health by observing how active it is at the pet shop. Stand back from the cage to avoid inhibiting the birds' natural behavior. The sassy birds that hop from perch to perch, whistling, always trying to boss the other birds around, are most likely males.

The plumage must be smooth, and no bare spots should be visible with the exception of the crown. The crown is devoid of feathers in all cockatiels, but in older birds is covered by surrounding plumage. Eyes must be clear and bright, free of any discharge or swelling. Nasal openings must not be clogged or runny. Respiration should be slow and even, not labored or irregular.

Study the droppings on the cage bottom. They are the best indicators of health. Droppings

Above: *While photographing this cockatiel, the photographer moved within one foot of the bird. Such calmness indicates that this bird had good potential for taming.* **Opposite:** *The author placing a lutino cockatiel on a training stand in preparation for advanced training lessons.*

should have good form, both dark green and white matter. Loose, watery droppings bright green in color indicate the presence of a digestive disorder.

Once you see a bird you like, examine him further when the pet shop employee removes him from the cage. Plan what you're going to look at to avoid restraining the bird any longer than necessary.

Does he have all his toes and claws? One missing toe or claw is no serious disability for the bird as long as no fresh wound or swelling is visible; however, do not purchase a bird with two or more missing toes or claws.

Feel the bird's chest to determine that he has good weight. A bird should be rejected if his breast bone protrudes sharply, indicating lack of weight and possible illness. Be sure to check the vent for any sign of soiling; a soiled bird should be rejected.

A lutino cockatiel preening itself. Healthy cockatiels will preen themselves regularly, keeping their plumage neat and clean.

Note the tight, clean feathers of this cockatiel's back. A healthy bird will have tight, even plumage.

Check the wings for lumps at the base of feathers. Make sure there are no sores or wounds anywhere on the body.

Any bird that sits fluffed up with his eyes closed or swollen, with discharge from the nostrils or soiled vent, should not be purchased, no matter how anxious you are to obtain a pet.

FOOD, FEEDING, AND CLEANING

For optimum benefit to your bird, a standard maintenance diet is best kept simple and balanced. Each day provide fresh sunflower seed, millet, oats, whole seed, parakeet or budgerigar seed, water with a commercially prepared vitamin supplement, and a portion of some green leafy vegetable such as wild lettuce, romaine, chicory, turnip tops, escarole, spinach, or carrot tops. They add important minerals and vitamins to the diet. Don't bother with iceberg (soft leaf lettuce). It

One of the real tests for a tame cockatiel is as follows: hold the tamed bird gently in your cupped hands.

Gently raise your upper hand so the bird is resting on your bottom hand without feeling restrained from flying away.

As soon as you feel the bird raise its body and prepare to fly away...

...you must quickly, but gently, replace your hand to restrain him from flying away.

Tame cockatiels will enjoy eating from their owners' hands.

has no food value. Wash the raw leaves and place them in the cage. If given regularly, green leafy vegetables will not cause diarrhea.

You may want to take some bird seed and sprout your own seedling grasses, which will be greatly appreciated by your pet and eaten with relish. If the seed you offer your birds does not sprout, it is not good food.

Other fruits and vegetables that can be given are corn, peas,

apple, orange, banana or just about anything that he enjoys. Keep in mind that your cockatiel may not accept fruits and vegetables immediately. It may seem that he never takes a nibble out of the green leafy vegetables that you provide. These should still be given regularly to allow him an opportunity to choose. Undoubtedly, he cannot acquire a taste for new foods if they are not available.

A good gravel mixture should be

provided in a separate dish. As an important source of minerals, gravel is wasted if used only on the cage bottom. A commercial gravel mixture is fine, but add a pinch of table salt whenever refilling the dish. Ask your pet dealer if he can get you grit and crushed oyster shell. Good quality grit is usually of organic origin and includes coral, barnacles, etc. Add these ingredients to the commercial gravel as follows: to a two-pound box of gravel (which, hopefully, contains a bit of charcoal), add one pound grit and one pound crushed oyster shell. This enriches the original mixture and is extremely important for breeding birds. In addition, cuttlebone or mineral block should always be present in the bird's cage.

Your bird will benefit from the following vitamin and mineral supplements; vitamins for the drinking water, oils for the seed, a few drops of cod liver or wheat germ oil given three times a week, and a powdered supplement to be sprinkled on fruits and vegetables. Your pet dealer will have these items for sale.

Once in a while you may want to treat your bird to some millet spray, an egg biscuit, or the seed toys made for budgies and parakeets.

Fresh branches from trees and bushes (such as oak, maple, citrus or other fruit trees, and hibiscus) are nourishing. Be absolutely sure that these have not been sprayed with insecticide or other chemicals. Rinse branches well in fresh water

Cockatiels will enjoy and will benefit from a varied diet. Seed alone will not provide your pet with all the nutrients it needs to remain healthy.

before giving to your cockatiel.

If you are buying a hand-fed baby, there may be additional dietary requirements. Find out from the dealer what the youngster was reared on. How long has he been weaned? Under no circumstances should you buy an unweaned baby! Weaning is perhaps the most difficult part of

Cuttlebone should be available to your cockatiel at all times, as you never know when your pet will feel the need for extra calcium.

Fruits and berries provide vitamins that may be lacking in a basic seed diet. Make sure, however, that such offerings are fresh and clean.

successfully hand-raising a cockatiel. Ask for the hatch date if available.

In the wild, cockatiels feed twice a day, in the morning and again in the afternoon. In captivity, most birds have food in front of them constantly. Owners feed their pets in the morning and leave the food all day. A newly acquired bird should have food available all day for at least two or three days, but as serious training commences,

you may want to initiate a feeding schedule. This is not to suggest that a bird be deprived of food, for no matter how training progresses, a cockatiel should be fed every day.

Feeding schedules refer instead to split rations, morning or afternoon feedings, or double feedings. Split rations can help to train the bird to accept food from your hand, do tricks, even speak. Take the normal amount of feed

Be sure that all seeds, grains, and sprouts come from safe sources. In addition, be certain that the seed has not gone stale.

that your bird consumes daily. Split it into three parts. Give one third before leaving for work in the morning. Use the next third during the training session when you get home. Give the rest, along with all remaining vegetables, when you are finished training for the evening. Always give some leafy vegetable in the morning, as the birds seem to eat most of it early.

If you are at home all day, split the rations into more parts. Do some training in the early morning before you feed him in his cage. Give him some seed in a dish at midday. Use seed every time you deal with the bird. Always be sure to give him enough to eat in the cage and time to eat it when you are finished training for the day.

Double feedings refer to double rations, usually necessary for breeding birds, very young babies and those recovering from illness.

If your new bird won't eat, don't

panic! Birds are usually upset by changes of environment, and one or two days without eating isn't very serious. You may want to check with the pet shop to see what previous diet the bird was given. Above all, don't constantly bother the bird. Give him an opportunity to settle down and accept his new surroundings.

When a cockatiel that you have had for some time suddenly stops eating, there is cause for concern. Observe him for any other behavioral changes. Consult a veterinarian. He will probably ask you to bring the bird to his office for examination. If he feels that your bird is not ill, he may recommend an appetite stimulant. Never wait too long before speaking to the vet if your bird stops eating. Due to their fast metabolic rate, weight loss can be extremely quick and possibly fatal.

It is useful to measure the

Sunflower seeds are popular with cockatiels, but, as they are fattening, do not offer your bird too many of them.

normal daily intake of your bird when he is in good health and eating well. Take a measuring cup and find out how much feed his dishes hold when full. If you fill them only half way, measure that amount. When refilling the seed dish, clean out the empty seed shells and measure the remaining amount. Subtract it from the total amount that you put in. This is his normal daily intake and is the amount that you should offer each day. Do not base the amount on your findings of just one or two days. Use one week or more to determine the bird's normal intake.

If your bird eats all that is offered, add a bit more the next day. A bird's appetite increases and decreases according to his physiological activities. During molting, for instance, the process of feather replacement can increase the nutritional needs of the bird. In cold weather, the need

If you keep more than one bird in a cage, be sure that both birds are eating enough. Sometimes, one bird may bully its cagemates when feeding time comes around.

Fresh water should be available to your pet cockatiel at all times. Commercially made water bottles and dishes are available at your local pet shop.

to produce body heat can increase the appetite. Ideally, you should remain flexible and learn to adjust the bird's diet as needed.

If your bird eats a good amount but appears to lose weight, definitely see your veterinarian. There are a number of possible causes, but don't try to diagnose your bird's problem unless you are willing to gamble with his continued good health.

Cleaning the bird cage and accessories should be done routinely. Each day scrub the water dish with hot water and soap. Use a bottle brush or sponge to remove any residue. Scrub the feed dishes at least twice weekly, more often if the bird defecates in or on them. Clean the cage bottom daily. Check the droppings, and the amount of feed, eaten and uneaten. For covering the bottom you can use newspaper or commercially prepared paper. In very large cages or outdoor aviaries, wood chips or sand might be more appropriate.

Perches should be cleaned with sand paper or a perch scraper to keep them free of food residues and feces. Never give your bird wet perches to stand on. Let them dry completely before replacing in the cage. Wet perches can lead to colds and arthritic conditions. Wash and dry the cage bottom once a week with hot water and soap. Clean and dry the bottom grill at the same time. Cage bars should be sponged off periodically with plain water to keep the cage shining and in tip-top shape.

Commercial bird sprays are fine to use on the cage, but use them sparingly on your indoor pet. Oil-base sprays should not be used on any cockatiel. If you feel that your bird has external parasites,

look for evidence. Horizontal marks running across the heavy wing and tail feathers usually indicate lice. Cover the cage with a white cloth at night to check for mites. They are usually attracted to the white cloth and will cling to it, showing up as very tiny little specks. It is unlikely that a cockatiel kept indoors would have a parasite infestation if you didn't bring the bird home with them, so don't automatically suspect "bugs" if your bird occasionally scratches. All birds scratch while preening. If their nose or head itches, they scratch, just like people. It is far easier to prevent bugs by keeping the cage clean and allowing your bird to bathe often in fresh water than to eradicate them once established.

Feather shine sprays should not be used on cockatiels.

Opposite: As you become acquainted with your new pet, you will learn its likes and dislikes, and you will be able to create a well-balanced diet that the bird will enjoy.

Equipment

Before bringing the bird home, have all the necessary equipment: feed, cage, extra cups and dishes, a cage cover, and training sticks and a stand, if you plan to use one. Set up the cage with food and water and choose a location for it. Decide on the primary trainer, the person who will tame the bird. Think of a few possible names for your bird and choose the one that seems appropriate. If you are planning to do speech training, a one or two-syllable name is recommended (such as Leo, Cleo, Mike, Mary, etc.). Three and four-syllable names may be too difficult for the bird to say.

Transport the bird from pet shop to home in a box with air holes cut in the sides. If you live in a cold climate, be sure to keep the bird warm while transporting him. It is best not to take a bird out in the rain, even in a box, for this

Left: Various types of bird feeders are available at your local pet shop. It may be a good idea to purchase one while you are buying the cage. **Opposite:** Have all necessary equipment ready for your new cockatiel's arrival. Preparation will go a long way in making your new bird feel at home.

Before placing a newly acquired bird in a cage with already established birds, a quarantine period should take place, as should a period of proper introduction.

increases the chance that he may catch cold. If possible, bring the bird home in the morning to give you the maximum amount of time to work with him the first day.

When buying a cage, look for standard heavy parrot wire, not light, thin budgie wire. Dimensions should be about 26 inches high, 20 inches wide and 20 inches deep. Get a metal cage in preference to a wooden or painted one. Metal cages last longer and are easier to maintain. Wooden cages won't hold cockatiels for very long, as they will chew right through them.

A bottom grill is advisable to keep the bird out of his own debris. Either wire or solid closed tops are fine. The door should be large enough to get your hand through with the bird on it without touching at any point. Birds are very nervous about moving through small doors on a hand.

Bells provide hours of entertainment. Just be sure that

Before your cockatiel arrives home, its cage should be in place and a taming area should be prepared.

the clapper is secure inside the bell. Mirrors should not be given to the bird if you expect him to speak. Ladders can be purchased made of both plastic and wood.

You may want to invest in an entire playground setup for your pet; ask your pet shop owner about it.

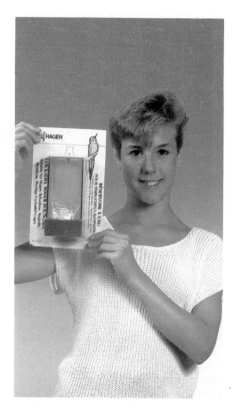

Left: Before bringing your pet cockatiel home, its cage should be furnished with feed and water dishes or dispensers. *Opposite:* Headstudy of a lutino cockatiel.

Taming

Before bringing your new bird home, consider the training area. Use a small room like the bathroom or hallway. This area is best isolated from the rest of the house. Cover wall mirrors and any large windows into which the cockatiel might fly. Trying to tame a bird in a living room or den can be an exercise in futility. The bird usually ends up on the curtain rods or under the couch. If the floor is tile, cover it to cushion any falls.

Clipping one of your cockatiel's wings to facilitate taming is recommended. Taming can be achieved without clipping the wing, but the bird has considerably more mobility. Clipping is not permanent, and once the bird is tame you can decide whether to reclip in the future (every five to six months) or

Left: Commercially prepared cockatiel treats are available at your local pet shop. These treats will come in handy as food rewards during taming and training sessions. *Opposite:* Some cockatiels have a fear of cage doors and may not come out when you offer your hand. If this is so, try to coax the bird out of the cage by offering it a stick.

After stick training has been accomplished, the next step is hand-training. The amount of time it takes for these steps varies from bird to bird.

let it fly. If you want to take the bird out in the yard, you must clip its wings and keep a close watch on the growth of new flight feathers. An indoor pet that flies loose must be protected from open doors. Hand-fed cockatiels do not need their wings clipped for taming purposes.

If you have decided to clip the bird's wing, ask the pet shop to help you with it before you take the bird home unless you are experienced and plan to do it yourself. It is best not to grab and restrain the bird too often. In addition, by clipping the bird at the shop, you avoid connecting the bad experience with the new surroundings. Clip only one wing. By clipping both wings you give the bird too much control over the direction of its flight. The bird is more quickly discouraged from attempting to fly if the flight pattern curves away from the chosen direction. Some people recommend that the wing feathers be plucked out instead of clipped. They reason that new feathers will grow in more quickly. This is true, but feather growth causes strain on the bird's system. The bird should be stressed as little as possible during the adjustment period, making clipping the preferred method.

Plan what you are going to do before beginning. You need good light, a pair of clippers (small wire cutters are perfect), scissors and styptic powder in case of bleeding. You must be able to recognize blood feathers from those that you can clip. Blood feathers are new feathers that are not finished growing in. They have blood vessels in the shaft to nourish the new feather as it grows and a direct line into the vascular system. Blood feathers must not be cut or clipped. Look at feather shafts carefully to make sure that you can identify any blood feathers that may be present.

Hold the wing firmly at the bend, and extend it to give a clear view of the primary and secondary flight feathers. The four long feathers on the end of the wing are the primaries. Leave the first two feathers as they are and cut the

Never take an unclipped cockatiel outside; however, if you must take your cockatiel outside, supervise it most carefully.

next two feathers in half with the scissors. Now take the clippers and clip the next eight to ten feathers at the point where the feather emerges from the shaft. Leave at least ¾ of an inch of feather shaft emerging from the wing. Before beginning to clip, push the undercoverts back to fully expose the feather shafts. Look at each feather before you clip it to be absolutely certain that it isn't a blood feather. Try not to cut the overcoverts to preserve

the appearance of the wing.

One very experienced person must clip the wing and another must hold the bird. The holder is responsible for watching the bird's respiration and holding the bird still. Use two hands to hold the bird. Put your thumb under the lower mandible, with the rest of your fingers around the head. Support the head and neck, keeping the neck straight. Don't pull the head or push it into the body. Don't let the body twist. Use

A pair of hand-tame cockatiels. Never try to tame two cockatiels at the same time, as the birds will distract each other and will accomplish little, if anything.

Getting your cockatiel to accept food from your hand is necessary for advanced training; therefore, it is a good idea to establish this practice as soon as possible.

your other hand to hold the bird's feet and torso.

Never hold a cockatiel by the tail; you'll end up with a handful of feathers! Support the bird's body on your lap or a towel-covered counter.

Occasionally you may want to clip the bird's claws. Natural wood perches help minimize the necessity, for they keep the claws nicely trimmed. It is best not to clip the claws on new arrivals unless they are overgrown or curled. Badly overgrown claws should be

clipped cautiously to avoid cutting the vein. By making certain that you work in good light, you should be able to see the vein through the claw. Have styptic powder ready in case you hit the blood vessel. Styptic pencil is too hard.

Take the clippers and just tip each claw. You can always take more off. If you hit blood, take the claw and dip it in styptic powder. You may have to pack it in with your fingertip. Be sure that the bleeding has stopped before you continue. Very tame birds will

A cockatiel that is kept by itself will become much more tame than one that is kept with other birds.

usually allow their owners to file their claws. This method is preferred to holding and clipping. File any rough edges from your cockies' claws so they don't catch in any material or your clothes. This could injure your cockatiel when it flies away.

Occasionally a bird's beak will become overgrown. With the right type and amount of chewing material, this rarely happens. The overgrown beak must be trimmed to prevent it from interfering with normal eating. Consult your vet for help with this problem.

From the first taming session to any advanced training that you may attempt, you will find food a helpful aid. Offer the bird food to help win its confidence. During taming, more seed will probably end up on the floor than in your bird's beak, but use it anyway. The cockatiel must learn to accept food rewards from your hand if you plan to try further training.

Commercially available millet sprays seem to be the big favorite with cockatiels. Cut the sprays into three-inch lengths for use during training sessions. Also offer sunflower seed. As you get to know your cockatiel better, you will discover which are its favorite foods. If possible, use these for rewards in advanced training.

Never use a leg chain on a cockatiel! Should the bird fight the chain, it could easily break its leg. You can accomplish the same goal (keeping the bird in one spot) by perch training and clipping the wing.

Toys will not be of much use in the initial taming sessions, but as your daily routine shapes up, they may become very useful. Playing with the bird with a bit of rope, leather or a bell can help develop a good rapport between you. The bird will consider your rings, earrings, necklaces and other jewelry as its personal playthings, as you'll soon discover.

Watching your cockatiel in front of the mirror can be very amusing.

Headstudy of a normal gray cockatiel. If your bird's beak should become overgrown, let the veterinarian trim it for you.

The bird whistles to its image, struts around and shows its wings to the beautiful bird in the mirror. However, mirrors distract the bird and should not be placed in its cage or near its stand.

Some birds become overly attached to the slight of their own image; they believe it is another bird and will try to feed, preen, and even mate with it. In some cases, the cockatiel's relationship with the "bird" in the mirror can undermine the one with its owner, as the bird prefers its avian "friend" to its human. However, these situations are rare, and as long as the cockatiel is not given a mirror as a permanent toy, no harm will be done. It may be a good idea to wait until the bird is completely tame before giving him a mirror.

HOW TO TAME THE COCKATIEL: THE FIRST HOUR

When you get the bird home,

The taming process can go a long way toward establishing a good relationship between you and your pet.

Save the box in which you brought your pet cockatiel home. It will come in handy for trips to the vet.

avoid commotion. The chosen trainer should stay with the bird, all others should go. Take it into the pre-designated training area. It is best to handle the bird before transferring it to the new cage. You may be able to tame it in the first session. Many cockatiels have naturally good dispositions, making taming a simple task.

Use a soft tone of voice to reassure the bird. Move slowly to let it see what you are up to. Never grab its body or pick it up from behind. Let the bird come out of the box onto the floor. Be certain that the floor is well cushioned against falls. This is very important and can save you a great deal of trouble. Be kneeling

Millet spray is a favorite of most cockatiels, and it makes a useful treat during training sessions.

down to greet the cockatiel as it ventures out of the box. Talk to it and offer your hand. If you want to use gloves, get the tight-fitting cotton or leather type. Large bulky gloves will scare the bird.

Work with the bird low to the floor at first to avoid having it take long falls. You can offer either your finger or your whole hand, fingers together, horizontal to its body. Push gently against its legs and body, just above the feet. The bird may step right on, or may try to fly or run away. When it settles down, kneel next to it and offer your hand again. Use your other hand to help block its escape attempts. It sometimes helps to work the bird from the corner of the room. The bird may hiss at you and try to bluff you by fluffing its feathers. Don't shy away if it tries these tactics or you'll never get past the first session.

If the bird bites, it usually can't

do too much damage. Do not hit the bird if it bites you. Tell it "No" in a loud voice and remove your finger from its beak if it is still there. If the bird persists in biting, take a piece of millet spray and put it right in its mouth as it tries to bite you. Keep working on getting it to step on your hand while you let it know that you're not afraid of its bite. This stage is critical. If the bird knows you're afraid, you are lost!

At this point it would be a good idea to remember your determination to tame your new cockatiel. Be patient, move slowly and persist in your efforts. When the bird steps on your hand, stay as still as you can. Don't try to move with the bird immediately. Let the cockatiel sit still, as it is probably panting to get rid of excess body heat. Birds do not have sweat glands, and excess body heat is expelled through the

Do not overtire your cockatiel. When you notice that the bird is getting restless, place it back in the cage for a rest.

respiratory system.

Talk softly to the bird and keep repeating its name. Try to touch it with your other hand. Move very slowly so that the bird hardly notices. Touch its feet first and just let your finger rest there for a minute. Move it up slowly until you are touching the feathers on its stomach. Wait. Talk to the bird. Bring the bird close to your body and keep it facing you, if possible, to block escape attempts. If you have to turn the bird around, gently touch its tail and it should turn.

Try to touch and pet its chest and chin, work your way up to the red earcoverts and its head. Once you can pet its head, you are just about done with the initial taming. Offer the bird some drinking water from its cup. It is probably hot and thirsty.

Try to have the bird step from one hand to the other. Give it a

Keep feed and water dishes out of the training area, as they will distract the bird. Only keep that food which you will feed to the bird from your hand.

If you plan to train your pet cockatiel, be sure that you are consistent in the amount of time you spend. Don't plan to work with your pet one day and skip the next.

slow drill on stepping from hand to hand. Try again to pet the bird. Be patient, move slowly and try to keep the bird facing you.

At this point you can either put the bird in its cage and wait until later or place it on a low stand, let it rest a few minutes and continue. You have now reached the end of your first hour with the cockatiel; it is the most difficult.

THE FIRST DAY

The trainer should arrange to spend the first day at home with the new cockatiel. If other birds are present in the house, keep the bird out of their sight and sound as much as possible. Continue to tame the bird in short intensive lessons. Practice having it step from the stand to your hand. Work with the bird in the same training

If you have children in your household, be sure they understand how to treat the cockatiel before they are allowed to handle it.

area as before. Keep its cage out of the training area. Encourage the bird to accept you and the stand as security objects, rather than the cage.

One of the most aggravating parts of training a bird is getting it out of and into the cage. If the cockatiel does not want to come out on your hand, see if it will come out by itself or on a stick.

As the bird begins to get used to the new surroundings, it will hop out of its cage whenever you open the door. Repeat the hand to hand training every time you take it out of the cage. Pet the bird as much as it will allow. Offer it millet. Talk to it and keep it with you as long as you want.

On the first day, try to accomplish stick training. Put the bird on the stand and approach it slowly with a short stick. Push against its legs gently to make it step up. Lift it off the stand and bring it over to you. Repeat this a few times. You may consider stick training an unneccessary task, but it comes in handy if the bird ever gets out of your reach, on the curtain rods or book shelves.

Continue these short lessons in a small area until you feel confident that you can walk into another room with the bird. You will learn to walk slowly and smoothly the longer you have a cockatiel riding on your hand or shoulder. When you are finished training for the day, put the bird in its cage. Give it its dinner and time to eat it before covering its cage for the night.

THE FIRST WEEK

The kind of routine that you develop with your bird in the first week is very important. If you work or go to school, feed and clean the bird in the morning. Take advantage of this time to talk to the bird and teach it its name. You should begin training lessons as

Mature children and cockatiels can forge meaningful relationships, but very young children are generally not ready for the responsibility a cockatiel entails.

soon as you get home to give maximum time to the bird each evening. Continue the regimen of the first day. Work on walking with the bird throughout the house. Let the bird perch on your shoulder if it so desires. Many cockatiels like to sit on your head.

Start training the bird to a high stand when you think it is ready. Use your judgment as to whether the bird will stay on the high stand or not. Choose a spot for the high stand in the room where you plan to spend the most time with your cockatiel. Like the cage, the stand must not be placed in a drafty or busy spot.

Introduce other family members to the cockatiel, one at a time, as soon as the bird has learned to step up on your hand. The other

When you attend to the bird's cage in the morning, talk to the bird and give it attention. Such a ritual will help the bird become accustomed to its new environment.

During the process of initial taming, keep toys out of the area and limit the equipment to a training stick and, perhaps, a training stand. Toys can be utilized in advanced training sessions.

family members can practice hand-training with the bird. Very young children need supervision, of course. When you are finished training for the night, put the bird in its cage, let it eat and cover its cage for the night.

THINGS TO REMEMBER

The more time you put into training the bird, the faster you'll get results. Use short lessons and deal with the bird often. Be

patient, move slowly. Cover all mirrors present in the training area. Begin taming the bird in a different room than its cage is in. Use a small room; cover the floor to cushion any falls the bird may take.

One trainer should tame the bird initially. Taming consists of stick, hand, perch and pet training. Other members of the family should get to know the bird as soon as it is hand-tame. Get the bird out of the cage and onto the stand as soon as possible.

When deciding on a trainer, choose a calm, patient person. The person who initiated the purchase of the bird or the one with the most time to devote to taming is the logical choice.

The daily routine should include feeding and cleaning. Scrub the water dish and supply fresh feed. Conduct the regular lessons, hand, stick and pet training. Give the bird free time on the stand (no lessons). Let it spend time with the family before putting it away for the night.

Left: The best way to make your cockatiel feel at home is to establish a routine and stick to it, as birds enjoy structure in their lives. *Opposite:* In lieu of a wooden dowel, stick training can be done with a Nylabird® dumbbell. These toys are available at your local pet shop.

Special Behavior Problems

Biting is the most obvious behavior problem that you may encounter. Birds bite because they are frightened or nervous. Perhaps they are older birds that have been mishandled, or never handled at all. If the bird bites, try stick training before hand-training. Never hit the bird or spray water on it. Use a loud "No" if it goes to bite you. Use millet to distract the bird.

Sometimes your bird will whistle for long periods of time. Usually it is trying to get your attention. The bird usually wants to come out or it hears other birds outside. When you want to stop your cockatiel from whistling, cover its cage. Remove the cover when the bird quiets down. Don't leave the bird covered when it is quiet.

Hissing is a normal response when the cockatiel is disturbed by the approach of strangers, if you peek under its cover once it is sleeping, or if you bother it while it's eating. This is a defensive

Left: A lutino cockatiel preening itself. Preening is a normal behavior, but feather plucking or chewing is a hazard to the bird's health. *Opposite:* Most cockatiels will respond to normal methods of taming and training, and they will adjust to life with their new family. However, remember that all cockatiels are individuals, and some will take longer than others to train.

posture which the bird is entitled to use.

Cockatiels are avid chewers. To keep your pet from chewing your important papers, school work, books, music, curtains, wallpaper and other household objects, perch train the bird to a stand. Give it plenty of chew toys to direct this normal activity. You will find that the cockatiel also chews up its own things: the paper that lines the bottom of its cage, its toys—and possibly its feathers. This is rarely a problem with a well-adjusted cockatiel. If you have provided a well-balanced diet, plenty of free time out of the cage and enough chewing material, you will probably never encounter a feather-chewing cockatiel.

Your bird may turn out to be an escape artist. A clipped bird is not too difficult to catch. Find the bird, and offer your hand or a stick if it

Since cockatiels are avid chewers, they should be provided with acceptable toys on which they can gnaw. Wooden perches and safe wooden toys are ideal.

Headstudy of a normal gray cockatiel. Some cockatiels may surprise you with their ingenious methods of escape. For this reason, it is a good idea to clip one of your bird's wings.

is tame. A wild bird with a clipped wing will try to run from you. If you have a bird net, net the bird and return it to its cage, unless you plan to do some training. A light towel thrown over the bird in the absence of a net will accomplish the same thing.

A flying bird is obviously more difficult to retrieve. Dim the lights, but don't make the room too dark. Shut doors to restrict its flight. Use

Your pet cockatiel should not be able to open the door of its cage. If the door is not constructed strongly enough, purchase an extra latch from your local pet shop.

your hand or a stick with a tame cockatiel. With a wild bird, a net is your best resort. It is easier on the bird and you. A towel is the second choice.

The cockatiel will take advantage of doors with easy-open latches to escape. Such doors must be repaired or given an additional latch. To prevent escape during initial taming sessions, isolate the training area. Structure the situation to give you optimum control. Avoid confusion.

Don't chase the bird :citedly.

If the cockatiel should get out the door into the yard, retrieve it as fast as possible with net, towel or gloves. If your bird flies into a tree, don't scare it out of the yard. Place its cage with food, water and millet spray in its clear view. If another cockatiel is available, place it in its cage next to the empty one as a draw. Wait. Hopefully, you will retrieve the bird successfully. Immediately take the bird indoors and clip it. If you prefer not to clip the wing, be much more careful in the future.

After a period of time and many daily lessons, you may decide that you have purchased an untamable cockatiel. Although this is highly unlikely, you may have a bird that is very nervous, or a biter. Cockatiels, like people, have many different personalities. Consider the problem carefully. If you have not adhered to the necessary training routine, there is no point in getting a different bird. If you have really tried to tame your cockatiel and failed, you may want to get another bird, a young one, and try again.

A good pet shop will trade in a bird which is untamable. Talk to the pet shop where you purchased the bird. Possibly, they will give

A pair of lutino cockatiels preening each other. Mutual preening is a sign that two birds have accepted each other. However, just as a cockatiel is capable of chewing its own feathers, it is also capable of pulling or chewing those of its cagemate.

you a partial credit toward another bird. Don't expect to be able to trade evenly for another cockatiel; that is unrealistic. At best, you can get your old bird a good home where it will fit in. Be prepared to spend more money for a new bird.

One-man birds are trained to be that way. The person that pays the most attention to the cockatiel is going to become its favorite person in the household. The same is usually true of your dog. It may allow the most intimate handling from that person and hold all others at bay. To avoid creating one-man birds, have all family members share the task of feeding and cleaning. Attention is the key. Those who feed the bird from their hands, offering it little treats like millet spray, are going to become its friends. Game playing also helps to establish a good relationship with the bird.

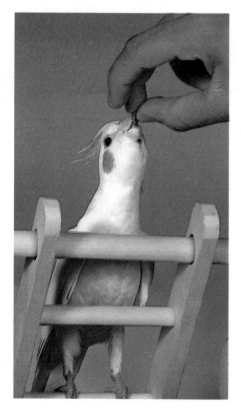

*Left: If you do not wish to create a one-man or one-woman cocka-tiel, be sure that all family members participate in caring for the bird after its initial training. **Opposite:** A lutino cockatiel inside an aviary.*

Training

There are definite differences between a tame bird and a trained one. Taming is the most basic form of training, consisting of stick training, hand-training and teaching the bird not to bite. A tame bird will not necessarily speak or let you pet it. This requires further training. A trained bird exhibits a greater variety of behaviors. These can be simple, but are usually complex behaviors that a tame bird has not learned.

How much and what kind of advanced training can you do with a cockatiel? Be realistic when you set goals for the bird. Speech training a cockatiel is realistic and worthwhile. Some birds develop a fairly extensive vocabulary. If you want a talking bird, try to purchase a male. Females can speak, but the male has more different natural sounds (listen to the songs it sings in the afternoon). Buy as young a bird as you can find.

When teaching the bird its first word, usually "Hello" or "Hi," speak slowly and distinctly. Enunciate the word. Work on "Hello" with the bird's name repeated after you say it. Work on only one new word at a time. The early morning and late afternoon,

Below: A lutino cockatiel in the process of being stick trained. **Opposite:** Wooden dowels are extremely helpful in taming, training, and even retrieving your pet cockatiel.

when birds sing their natural songs, is a good time to try speech training. You can give the bird its lesson inside or outside the cage. You can use a recording or teach the bird in person. If you want the bird to talk on command, you should teach in person and reward for every correct response. Recorded lessons can be made at home on cassettes of your own voice, or bought commercially. A woman or child makes the best speech trainer for a cockatiel. Their voices are closer to the natural pitch of the bird's voice. When speaking to your cockie, try to imitate this shrill voice.

Once your cockatiel has learned to say "Hello," you can go on to a short phrase such as "How are you?" Be sure to work on only one word or phrase at a time. The bird must be fairly fluent with one word or phrase before you begin teaching new material.

Although speech training isn't usually associated with cockatiels, a few birds may learn a word or two.

When speech training your cockatiel, stand in front of the bird, look it in the eye, and repeat the word or phrase slowly and clearly.

Understand the difference between responsive and imitative speech. Responsive speech means that the bird will respond a certain way to a given cue. You say, "What's your name?" and the bird replies, "Leo." Imitative speech means that the bird will repeat what you say to it. You say, "Hi," and the bird replies, "Hi."

You must keep the bird clipped if you plan to take it outside. Don't leave the bird outside by itself on a perch. (Think of cats!) When you first begin to take the bird into the yard, stay a good distance from any tall trees. Be sure that none of

the neighborhood pets will jump at your bird and scare it off of its perch. Begin by taking the bird outside when it is quiet; place it on its stand. Stay near and watch how it adjusts to the new surroundings. Make the first visits outside fairly short. When you have trained the bird sufficiently to stay outside for longer periods, never leave your cockatiel in direct sunlight. Give the bird shelter from the breeze. On very warm days (over 72°F), it is fine to give your bird a spray bath outside.

Training your cockatiel to sit on a stand may be some of the most

Ladders, swings, and playgrounds can be utilized in your training program. Such toys and cage furnishings are available at your local pet shop.

valuable training that you do. Place the bird on the stand. If the bird jumps off, get it with your hand or a stick and put it back on. Repeat this as often as needed until the bird gets the idea.

Reward the bird when it sits well. By outfitting the stand with some toys, you can make it more attractive to the bird.

Trick training a cockatiel requires that you understand the

basics of a reward system. Reward the bird for desired behaviors; ignore, don't punish, undesired behaviors. Use food and praise to reinforce your bird's successful response. Reward for each repetition of the desired behavior.

Be realistic when deciding on a trick to teach. Cockatiels can learn to climb ropes and ladders. They can retrieve seed from a hanging cup, or place objects in a container. Train the bird to ring a bell for a seed reward. Don't expect to teach your cockatiel to ride bicycles or roller skate. This is unrealistic. (But if you graduate to a larger parrot, Ah...!)

Give your bird short lessons, three to five minutes, as often as you like, but don't tire it. Teach only one trick at a time. End your lesson before your bird stops attending to it. Try to end on a high point; praise and reward the bird.

The best way to decide on a trick to teach is by capitalizing on your bird's natural antics. Your pet might display his wings and tail feathers. Train it to do this on command. See if the bird will roll over in your hand, unusual for a cockatiel, but possible! As you get to know your bird, watch for

Trick training your cockatiel can be a rewarding experience for both you and your bird if you are patient and consistent.

individualized behaviors. Use these to shape a training schedule for your cockatiel.

Once you begin training, be certain to repeat the lessons every day. Trick training the bird on weekends, or twice a week, is a waste of time and frustrating for both you and the bird.

Below: A hand-tame normal gray cockatiel. *Opposite:* Chains can be utilized in a cockatiel training program, as cockatiels love to climb and play on them. Be sure, however, to get a chain of the proper size. An unsafe chain is a dangerous toy.

One of the first lessons that you must learn as a bird owner is that accidents can happen. They can happen in the taming process. A bird that has the freedom of the house can have run-ins with other family pets, large picture windows, or mirrors. You could come home to find your pet cockatiel twisted in a toy that you once thought was safe.

First of all, don't panic. A smart bird owner should acquaint himself with useful first aid preparations. By all means seek the advice of a veterinarian for follow up care, but in some situations you must act quickly.

Use hydrogen peroxide to stop bleeding and as an antiseptic to clean wounds. Get some styptic powder from your pet shop. Styptic powder is especially useful to stop bleeding when clipping claws, or if your bird should break a blood feather. Buy a commercial bird salve to dress cuts. Petroleum jelly is a good salve, but be sure

Left: A pair of lutino cockatiels. *Opposite:* The best way to keep your cockatiel healthy and safe is to prevent accidents and illness by offering safe, clean surroundings.

If you house two or more cockatiels together, keep a close eye on the birds for any signs of illness. Contagious diseases can decimate an aviary.

not to spread it all over the bird. It takes a long time to wear off the feathers. Also available at the pharmacy is antiseptic powder. Used to sprinkle on open cuts, it also helps to stop bleeding. Buy these medications and keep them on hand in the medicine chest. Have a veterinarian's phone number in your telephone book so that you won't have to search for it in an emergency. Act first, then call the vet!

If your bird cuts himself, clean the wound off with hydrogen peroxide. Stop the bleeding by holding a cotton swab with peroxide against the wound. Sprinkle with antiseptic powder or use a bird salve to dress the wound. Never cover the cut with tape or bandage. This will only irritate the bird, who will pull it off anyway.

If you suspect that your cockatiel has broken a leg or wing, keep the bird quiet and warm. Remove all high perches from the cage. Put food and water within easy reach. Restrict the bird's activity and speak to your vet. Avoid moving a bird having any suspected broken bones. As with wounds, binding the area does little good.

A bird with a broken leg is smart enough to favor the leg while it heals. Most birds mend well if given a good diet and left undisturbed during convalescence. Broken wings usually droop down on the body or angle up unnaturally. Don't try to set the wing. Let it hang loose and talk to the vet. He will probably recommend leaving it the way it is, unless the break is extremely severe, twisting the wing out in a bad position. Again, the bird will favor the injury while it heals. Restrict the bird's activity and give plenty of food, vitamin and mineral supplements, and fresh green leafy vegetables.

Broken or clipped claws that bleed should be dipped in styptic

A lutino cockatiel. If your pet is allowed free time out of its cage, be sure to supervise it closely. It is too easy for a cockatiel to injure itself needlessly.

FIRST AID

powder. Use hydrogen peroxide if you don't have styptic powder. Put the bird in its cage and leave it alone. If the bleeding continues at a fast rate, you may have to grab the bird again and pack the bleeding claw with the powder. Put the bird down as soon as possible, for a struggling bird's heart beats faster than one sitting quietly in a cage.

Treat a broken blood feather the same way, with styptic powder. Sometimes a broken blood feather must be pulled, because every time the bird flaps its wings it bleeds. Seek the help of an experienced person or a vet to pull out blood feathers, unless you have done it or been shown how to do it. Refrain from looking at the bird constantly to allow him to rest while the blood congeals.

Suspect illness if your daily check on the bird's droppings reveals bright green, brown or loose, watery droppings—not just one or two bad droppings, but a whole day's worth. Watch for any sudden decrease in appetite. A bird that sits fluffed up, sleeping all day, should visit the vet for an examination.

Birds with colds have the same symptoms as people with colds. They sneeze, not once or twice while preening the feathers, but often, possibly accompanied by nasal discharge. The eyes may become red and inflamed. The bird may cough and wheeze. After a complete examination, your vet will probably prescribe an antibiotic and possibly an ophthalmic ointment for sore eyes.

The most often recommended antibiotics are tetracycline and its derivatives, and chloromycetin. Never give your bird an antibiotic drug prescribed for people. Although the drug might have the same name, the dosage for a person could easily kill your cockatiel. Always let your vet prescribe the kind and dosage of any medication given to the bird.

You must keep the bird very warm when it is ill; 90-95°F is about right. Cover the cage and use a strong, light heater to radiate heat. Monitor the temperature with a thermometer. Most cockatiels are strong enough to throw off a simple cold, but if you fail to detect and treat it, the simple cold can become much more serious. Respiratory conditions such as asthma, pneumonia, aspergillosis and chronic sinus infections usually begin as colds. These conditions are difficult to treat and are often fatal.

It is best to prevent serious illness by scrubbing the water cup, cleaning the cage bottom, and checking the droppings daily. Also, provide fresh seed, fruit and vegetables, as well as the necessary vitamin and mineral

Opposite: A cockatiel's health shows in its eyes, plumage, and its attitude toward its owner and/or cagemates.

supplements. House the bird out of drafts and don't keep it up all night to entertain your friends.

Psittacosis, a respiratory disease, is extremely rare in caged house pets. Caused by viral agents, the symptoms resemble atypical pneumonia. Psittacosis may occur when birds are housed in crowded, dirty cages and fed an inadequate diet with foul water. This is rarely the case with a house pet. All birds imported into the United States must be quarantined for psittacosis and other diseases, assuring that the birds passed through are free of the disease. For this reason, you should never buy a bird that may have been smuggled into the country. The price might seem right until you discover illness in your new pet. Buy all birds from reputable pet dealers. If your pet cockatiel develops a severe cold, do not suspect psittacosis. Take the bird to the vet as soon as illness is noticed.

Sinus trouble is indicated by swollen, red eyes and a discharge from the nostrils. If left untreated, the bird could develop a sinus

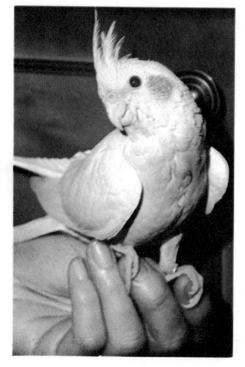

A lutino cockatiel. Keep an eye on your pet's eating habits and weight. If your cockatiel seems to eat enough yet is losing weight, take it to the vet at once.

Never place poisonous plants, like this poinsettia, within reach of a cockatiel. Many household plants can be deadly to your pet.

knot on its forehead, and the condition may continue to worsen. Your vet will probably prescribe the same antibiotic medications that he uses to treat colds. Again, keep the cockatiel warm and quiet.

Whenever your bird is ill, offer it as much to eat as it wants. If the bird gets picky, offer it its favorite foods and let it eat as much as it can. Although a balanced diet is important when your bird is sick, it is more important that it eats plenty.

Digestive disorders may accompany colds or appear by themselves. Constipation is indicated by droppings devoid of green fecal matter. All the droppings show as white and clear matter. Diarrhea is more prevalent than constipation. Usually diarrhea is a symptom of some other illness. Sometimes a bird will stop passing waste material completely. This is extremely serious, for, without treatment, the bird's entire system will be poisoned rapidly. When you suspect any digestive disorder, go over the diet that you have been giving and seek advice from a qualified vet.

Going light refers to weight loss and usually indicates some other disorder. Try to rule out worm infestation as the cause of weight loss by providing the vet with a fresh stool sample to examine. Adjust the diet to provide more fattening foods like oats and more sunflower than parakeet seed. Offer milk-soaked wheat bread as

A healthy cockatiel should have clear nostrils. Clogged nostrils indicate a cold or a more serious ailment which should be treated by a veterinarian.

Two or more parrots kept together will generally keep each other occupied. If you keep a single parrot, however, be sure to spend ample time with the bird. If you don't, it will be bored and may become distraught or destructive.

well as corn kernels. The bird's dietary requirements may be changing. Ask your vet for an appetite stimulant if you think it necessary.

Feather problems rarely occur with a happy, well-fed cockatiel. An unusually heavy, constant molt is a definite feather problem. Check the diet, and make sure that you are not artificially overheating your bird. Sometimes birds chew their feathers. This may be as a result of a poor diet or a high level of anxiety.

Ingrown feathers appear as lumps that begin at the base of the feather follicles and grow larger as the feather grows and tries to push out. Ingrown feathers must be treated by experienced people or your vet. Occasionally, a double feather grows on the wing or tail. There is no cause for concern unless the double feather bleeds. Usually the double feather grows out properly and eventually drops out in a molt. It may or may not grow back the same way.

Tumors, lumps and bumps can occur anywhere on the bird's body. They can be on the skin or internal. If you suspect a tumor, take the bird to the vet. It may be fatal, but usually is not. The vet may choose to remove the tumor. Many tumors grow to a certain size and do not seem to affect the bird's general health for years. Sinus knots are often mistaken for tumors by inexperienced bird owners.

Foot problems and lameness can occur in both young and old birds. Arthritis and rheumatism can be caused by making the bird sit on wet perches, or on perches too small to give him a proper grip. Arthritic birds must be kept warm and given perches of differing shapes and diameters. Make sure the diet is well balanced and supplemented.

If your bird appears to be lame or have a sore foot, it may help to soak the affected area in warm water for five minutes. Better yet, hold the bird's bad leg under warm running water. Use a light stream of water, not too warm, and try not to get the bird wet all over. When five minutes have passed, dry the leg gently and paint with iodine or mercurochrome. Don't cover the area with any sort of bandage. Call your vet and tell him the

symptoms and how you have treated them. He may suggest a different sort of first aid. Again, check the content of the bird's diet. Green leafy vegetables and vitamin and mineral supplements are very important if your bird comes up lame.

Occasionally, a bird develops paralysis. This may be due to a nervous system disorder. Keep the bird warm and place food and water within easy reach. See your vet as soon as possible.

Shock is a very serious condition that can occur as a result of injury. The bird stops moving and may make plaintive crying sounds or be silent. The eyes fail to focus and breathing becomes shallow. Immediately place the bird in a warm, protected spot. You may want to wrap the bird in a small towel or wash cloth. Don't continually fuss with the bird, as it needs warmth, quiet, and rest. Put food and water within reach, although it may be some time before the bird tries to eat or drink. If the condition is a result of injury, apply first aid before placing the bird in its cage

Opposite: A lovely lutino cockatiel. Natural wood branches make good perches, but since it is almost impossible to tell whether a tree has been sprayed with dangerous chemicals, your best bet would be to purchase some of the many types of perches available at your local pet shop.

A sick cockatiel must be isolated from healthy birds, and many times the veterinarian will recommend that the bird be placed in a hospital cage. These special cages are available for sale or rent at pet shops.

or, if you think it warmer, a small box. Warmth is imperative for a bird in shock.

Concussion resembles shock symptomatically. Usually the result of the bird flying head first into windows, walls, or mirrors, first aid treatment is the same as for shock. Try to prevent this by providing your flying cockatiel with a safe place in which to fly. Avoid large windows and mirrors in the flying space. Concussion can be

fatal, so it is better to protect your bird than to treat the condition.

Eggbinding can occur in single and breeding female birds. Poor diet and insufficient exercise can cause the condition. Treatment can take various forms. Keep the bird very warm and quiet. If your cockatiel is tame, apply two or three drops of mineral oil to the vent. Don't try to push the egg out unless you have had previous experience, for it is fatal if the egg breaks inside the bird. Speak to your vet and ask his advice.

Some female cockatiels, like chickens, lay eggs on a regular schedule, even in the absence of a mate. Give the bird plenty of flying time and a diet rich in minerals. Egg production causes a strain on the system, and if mineral content in the diet is insufficient, the bird will draw on her own body calcium to make eggs. A well-fed bird that gets plenty of exercise can pass eggs regularly with no harm. Try to distract the bird by giving her more attention. Above all, be certain that the diet is well-balanced and the bird is not becoming weak from the strain of egg laying.

RESUME

Remember, a sick bird is best left in a warm, quiet cage. Don't drag your bird to the vet for every little sneeze. Call and consult him for advice before you show up at his office. He will tell you if he

For safety's sake, do not house your cockatiel with birds of other species. A few birds may get along, but most will not.

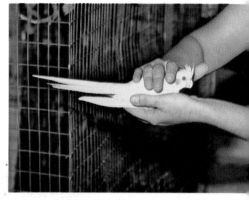

Opposite: A trained cockatiel will allow you to hold it in your hand without biting or trying to escape. **Above, top left:** In order to train the bird to stay in your hand, hold the bird gently but firmly. **Above, top right:** If the cockatiel wriggles, hold it against your body until it settles down. **Above, lower right:** Extend your hands away from your body. **Above, lower left:** Finally, slowly release your grip.

wants to see the bird. It is far better to prevent illness by keeping the bird's cage clean and its diet balanced. Treatment is much more difficult and time consuming than preventive maintenance. Never administer drugs to your cockatiel without first consulting your vet. Don't wait long to consult the vet if your bird is losing weight or shows definite cold symptoms. Before you get to the vet, keep the bird very warm (90 to 95°F) and quiet. When transporting him, try to avoid sudden temperature changes. To repeat, a clean cage and good diet are the most important elements in preserving your bird's continued well-being.

One of the main advantages of buying your cockatiel from a pet shop or bird store is the availability of reliable, experienced advice, as well as emergency equipment.

A hospital cage is usually available for rent or purchase from a pet shop that handles a lot of birds. This is a small cage which has a built-in heat source. It is mostly closed in to prevent drafts and to cut down the amount of light entering from outside the cage, so as not to get the sick cockatiel excited. Ask your pet shop about the availability of a hospital cage the next time you visit it for seed, so you will know what is available to you.

If you have more than one bird, you might consider buying your own quarantine cage. You'll want to use it for isolation and observation of newly acquired cockatiels (or any other bird for that matter) and for restraining and treating injured cockatiels.

Opposite: A lovely stick trained pearly cockatiel. The health of a pet cockatiel depends greatly upon the care it receives from its owner.

Opposite: *The author with a lutino cockatiel. At first, this bird bit Ms. Teitler every time it was given the chance, but was tamed within 15 minutes.* **Above:** *It is never safe to allow a pet cockatiel to have complete liberty, especially when the bird is out of doors. Always supervise your pet, whether it has had its wings clipped or not.*

Breeding

People who enjoy their cockatiels as pets often consider attempting to breed them. First, be aware that breeding birds are not usually tame to their owners once they begin rearing a family. Often, the most affectionate pets turn into aggressive, possessive parents. If possible, keep a single pet and buy other cockatiels for breeding.

Never breed related birds. Although some people feel that related pairs produce good offspring, it is genetic fact that flaws can be compounded and passed on. Young birds may attempt to nest and breed, but two-year-old birds are more reliable. Try to determine if you are getting mature birds in good physical condition.

Breeding cockatiels should be accustomed to a well-balanced diet before you get them. Otherwise you should delay their nesting until they have been on a

Left: A pair of cockatiels outside their nestbox. Nestboxes are available at your local pet shop.
Opposite: Breeding cockatiels is a challenge, but it is also a great responsibility.

Opposite: Stick training is a most sensible method of taming your cockatiel. The cockatiel often feels more secure with a stick perch available to it. *Above:* Holding the bird should be part of the daily training session, as the bird must become accustomed to such handling when it goes to the vet or has its nails trimmed.

proper diet for five to six months. This is to ensure that your hen will not become eggbound from poor nutrition. The parents may not feed the babies sufficiently if they have not been eating well prior to nesting. Nesting, egg laying, and rearing young stress the breeding bird's system. Poor nutrition could cause illness in the breeding pair, infertile eggs and deserted or sickly offspring.

The breeding cage must be large enough to allow the birds to fly across lengthwise. Good dimensions are four feet high, four feet long, two to three feet wide. The cage should be placed in a quiet location. Too much interference can discourage the birds from breeding. The breeding box should be placed in the cage so that you can observe the progress of the babies once they hatch.

Don't constantly bother the birds, but after you begin to hear sounds from the nest, you should check once a day to be sure that inexperienced parents are properly feeding the young. If not, you may have to hand-feed to keep the babies alive. Try to avoid hand-feeding. Parent-raised babies develop faster, grow larger and seem to be a bit hardier than hand-reared young.

Nestboxes can be made out of wood or cardboard. Wood lasts longer, but there is some

A group of various colored cockatiels. Breeding for the different cockatiel color varieties is just one interesting aspect of this vocation.

A pair of lutino cockatiels in the act of preening each other. Mutual preening is often a sign that a pair is getting ready to mate.

advantage to being able to dispose of used boxes after each season. At the beginning of the next season, you can replace with new boxes of the same kind. Good dimensions are 12 inches high, 16 inches long and 12 inches wide. Cut the door in the lower left-hand corner of the box, three inches from the bottom. The door should be big enough to allow the birds to pass through easily, but small enough to give them privacy inside the box. They will make adjustments to your design by chewing in their own architectural ideas.

Also, cut some ventilation holes on three sides of the box. The top of the nestbox should open halfway to give you access to the inside. Should you need to take the babies, such access is imperative.

Cover the bottom of the box with wood shavings. Use pine bedding, but don't use cedar. Some birds will nest in cedar but

Above: A four-day-old baby cockatiel with a crop that is full of seed. *Opposite:* A young hand-fed cockatiel. As soon as a hand-fed baby comes out of the nestbox, it should be placed on a perch for training. Hand-fed cockatiels become very tame; however, they are usually not as hardy as those reared by the parent birds.

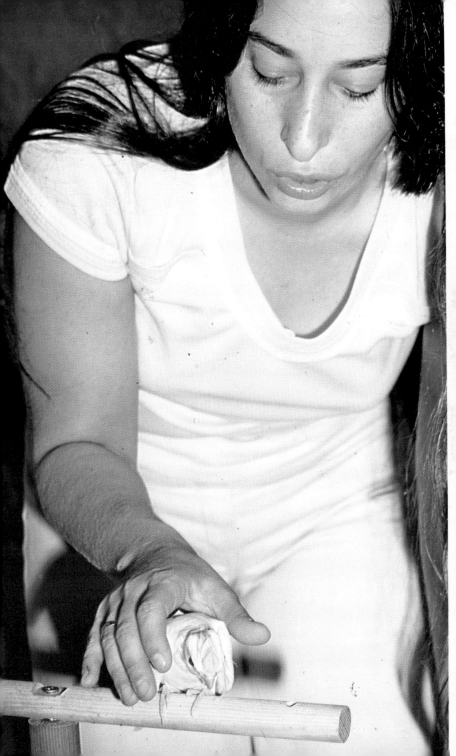

A pair of lutino cockatiels. Normal gray cockatiels are generally considered to be hardier than those of other colors; however, the type of the other varieties has improved in recent years.

pine shavings are preferred. Attach a nest frame to the rear right-hand side of the box. Use one-inch by one-inch or two-inch by two-inch wood to make a nest frame. This will keep the eggs from rolling around in the box and getting chilled. The frame also keeps the babies close to one another, under the sitting parent. This helps keep the babies' temperature constant and high.

Use the same dimensions and design for a wooden nestbox. Put hinges in the top to give you access to the inside of the box. At the start of each season, thoroughly clean and bug-spray the box. Allow 24 hours after spraying before introducing the box to the birds. Put wood shavings in the bottom to a depth of 2½ inches. Be certain that your ventilation holes are adequate.

Wood boxes are warmer than cardboard. Clean out the inside of the box once a week after the babies hatch, unless the parents are too disturbed. Don't change all the shavings, just try to remove any fungus or mold that may be growing on the droppings of the young birds. If the parents react too badly to the cleaning by biting you and trampling on the babies, don't persist. You could cause more harm than the fungus!

Most cockatiels like to breed in the autumn. Summertime in the hot climates is too hot for breeding your birds. Indoor breeding with temperature artificially controlled can be accomplished year round. Before the breeding season arrives, begin giving the potential parents an enriched diet. Replace the bird's gravel with a fresh mixture. Check every week to see if more gravel is needed. Mineral block or cuttlebone must be supplied. Fresh branches should be given often. Offer much more soft food, including corn kernels, peas, green leafy vegetables and

Breeding cockatiels should be given additional access to cuttlebone, as their need for calcium increases greatly during this period.

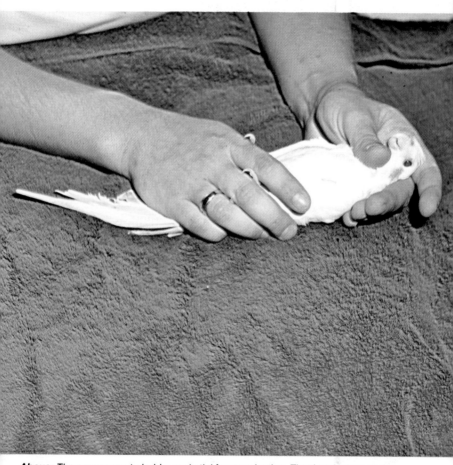

Above: *The proper way to hold a cockatiel for examination. The thumb goes under the lower mandible (beak), while the other fingers cradle the head. The other hand holds down the rest of the body, including the feet.* **Opposite, top and bottom:** *If you wish to examine the wings, get a second person to help you. The second person should hold the wing out carefully, placing the thumb at the joint of the wing and then extending the feathers.*

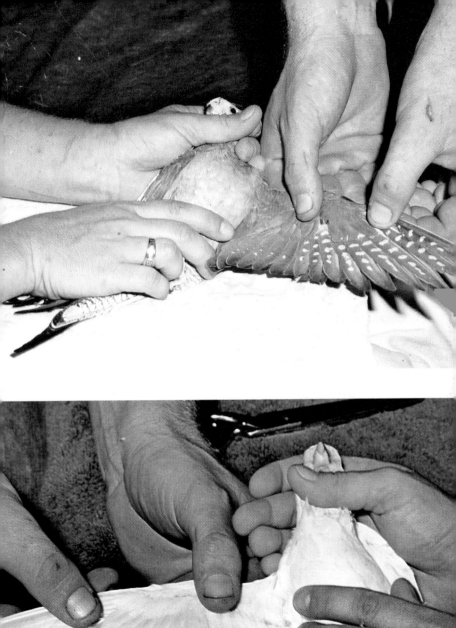

bread. Bread can be made by toasting whole wheat bread and crumbling it into a dish. Add sunflower or millet meal and cod liver oil to the crumbled bread. Mix these ingredients together, adding some warm water to make it soft and crumbly. Don't add too much water or the mixture will become mushy and the birds won't eat it. Some cockatiels refuse to eat bread, but try to offer it anyway.

By all means give them the vegetables and fruits that they will accept, but continue to provide bread on a daily basis. Don't let the bread sit overnight. Prepare fresh bread each morning for feeding parents.

Be certain that the vitamin regimen is complete. Administer these daily instead of two to three times a week.

The breeding birds must be able to fly within the breeding cage. Exercise is imperative for breeding birds. Consider exercise as important as a good diet. Lack of exercise is another cause of eggbinding, infertile eggs, and added stress during breeding.

When you want to begin the breeding season, place the nestbox inside the birds' cage. Go away and leave the birds alone to investigate. Every day feed and clean the birds, and give them complete privacy the rest of the time. Be patient. Once they begin to customize the nestbox and the hen begins to consume a great deal of gravel and mineral block, it

is just a matter of time before the first eggs arrive.

It may take four to six weeks for the birds to get started, but usually the pair gets to work immediately. Expect three to five eggs to a clutch. The eggs will be layed every other day and take 18 to 21 days to hatch. An indication that the hen has layed will show in the inordinate amount of droppings deposited on the bottom the cage. The birds take turns sitting on the eggs. Usually the hen sits from dusk to dawn and the cock from dawn to late afternoon, when the two of them spend some time together before the hen goes in for the night. Many pairs sit together on the eggs and the babies.

When the babies begin hatching, you will hear sounds from the nest. Soft peeping from the babies as the parents feed them is a good indication of a successful hatching. The parents feed tiny amounts of food at first, but soon begin stuffing the babies until the crop appears to be distended. A well-fed baby cockatiel looks overfed to the inexperienced eye. If the crop is stuffed with hard seed, the babies will not develop rapidly and may not derive the necessary nutrition

Opposite: Before breeding any two cockatiels, one must determine that the birds are in excellent health and that they are genetically compatible in order to produce offspring of the desired type.

Above and opposite: Clipping a cockatiel's wing requires some experience. Let your pet shop dealer or veterinarian demonstrate the proper way to do this at first.

from the parents' regurgitated food. If you see hard seed in the crop, be sure to offer green leafy vegetables liberally and plenty of soft bread.

The babies grow rapidly when fed properly and may be poking their heads out of the nest at four weeks of age. Pinfeathers appear at about seven days to cover a nearly naked body. The heavy wing, tail, and crest feathers appear first. Then pinfeathers begin to cover the crop, back and abdomen.

The first time that you see the babies outside of the nest is a thrill. The babies feel the same way and usually run back to the security of the box as soon as they see you. In a couple of days they get used to you and begin flapping their wings on the outside of the box. Prior to leaving the nest box, the babies practice flapping on the inside, making lots of noise that you will soon learn to recognize as baby exercise.

Babies leave the box for good at five to six weeks of age. They are still fed by the parents, but weaning begins immediately. The parents by then may already have more eggs in the nest. By eight weeks of age, most babies are eating independently and can be separated from the parents. Some cockatiels take longer to wean than others, especially if the parents are inexperienced. Be sure that the babies are eating on their own when you separate them

from the parents, or they may lose weight and become ill. At ten weeks, the babies can usually go to new homes to be tamed as family pets. Ten-week-old cockatiels are not old enough to travel to the pet shop for resale.

Be sure to interrupt the breeding season after two clutches by removing the nestbox.

Deserted or abused offspring may have to be hand-reared. By all means, encourage the parents to raise the young, but if this is not possible, set up an incubator and stabilize the temperature at 95°F before placing the babies in it. Handle baby cockatiels as little as possible, take them out for feeding and replace them in the incubator before they get chilled. A baby with no feathers cannot maintain its body heat for long.

Wrap one baby bird at a time in a towel and feed according to the following schedule: a one to four-day-old baby every two to three hours round the clock; a five to nine-day-old every four hours. At ten to 14 days you can stretch the feedings to six hours. Continue at six-hour intervals for the remainder of hand-feeding. Fill the crop up and try to keep air out. You can gently push out excess air, but don't squeeze the chick. Feed with a very small spoon. It is almost impossible to overfeed. Use the bread mixture, warmed and softened with water. Add more sunflower meal than you would for the parents, but

Before pairing off two cockatiels, it is a good idea to let them become safely acquainted at first.

remember that it is concentrated. Add some prepared baby peas or green beans to replace the green leafy vegetables. Almost any formula that is well balanced and soft enough for the baby to take easily will be useful for hand-rearing.

Begin weaning the babies at seven to eight weeks of age. Hand-reared young usually remain dependent longer than parent-raised. Feed the babies in the morning and place sunflower seed, parakeet seed, millet spray,

water and a portion of their formula in a dish on the bottom of the nursery cage. You will have to switch from the incubator to the nursery cage when the babies begin to fly. In the late afternoon, before covering the babies for the night, give them a good feeding by hand. Never put the babies to sleep without feeding them their full.

Continue to wean the babies in this manner and soon you will see cracked seeds on the cage bottom. At this point offer green

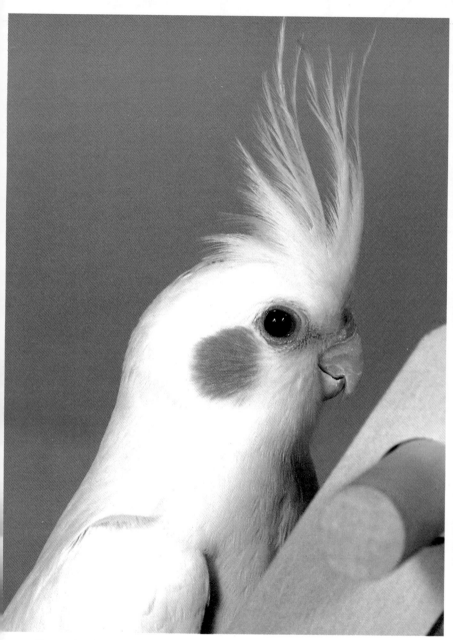

Above: A pair of normal gray cockatiels. *Opposite:* Cockatiels are rather easy to sex once they have fully matured, as the coloration of the male and female are visibly different.

leafy vegetables in addition to the other feed and formula. By ten weeks you should be able to let the babies eat on their own all day and feed them just one time a day, in the afternoon. Watch the babies' progress. Baby cockatiels progress at their own individual rate. Adjust the schedule to fit the needs of the situation, but never skip feedings because it is inconvenient for you. If that is the case, better not try hand-feeding. Give the babies to someone who can raise them if you don't have the time.

Breeding cockatiels can be enjoyable or heartbreaking. Be certain that you will accept the confinement that breeding birds often means. If you are accustomed to an active social life, it is best to stick with a single pet, or you may find yourself in the uncomfortable position of deciding whether to let a baby bird live or die. Often, the breeding is unsuccessful. If you cannot take disappointment or if you are impatient, don't try breeding.

Breeding cockatiels can be a rewarding experience, but it is not a step to be taken lightly. Plan well before establishing any breeding program.

Index

A white, or lutino, cockatiel and a normal male cockatiel.

Taming and Training Cockatiels
KW-001